The Little

What it Means to be Born Again...

**Written and Illustrated
by
Tempe Brown**

ISBN: 9781503004559

Printed in the United States of America

DEDICATION

I humbly dedicate this book to my three children, April, Melinda and Tommy. I only wish I had a little book like this to read to you when you were small. How different our lives would have been.

Yet, in His infinite wisdom, He chose to let each of us find Him in our own way and I praise Him for bringing us all to a place where we could be birthed into His kingdom.

And cats like to hang out with cats.

And people like to hang out with people.

6

But God is a Spirit.[1] Who do you suppose
God wants to hang out with?

That's right!

But God had this problem because
He made these little dirt people.

Can you imagine trying to fellowship
with a little clod of dirt?

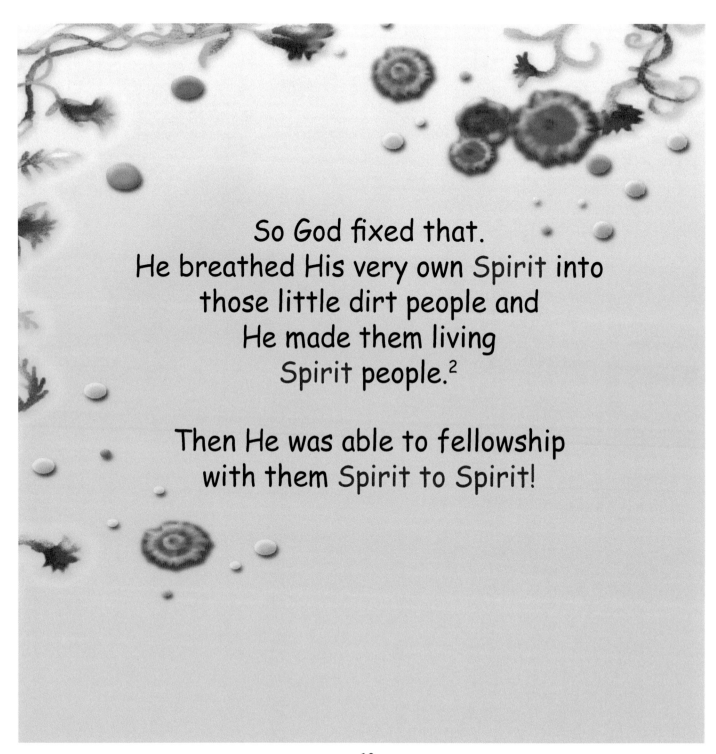

So God fixed that.
He breathed His very own Spirit into
those little dirt people and
He made them living
Spirit people.[2]

Then He was able to fellowship
with them Spirit to Spirit!

He had made a beautiful garden for them to live in, and He said, "You may freely eat of every tree in the garden except the one in the center of the garden.

If you eat of that one, you shall surely die."[3]

The devil (the Bible calls him a serpent) tricked them into eating of it, but they didn't keel over and drop dead.[4]

WHAT DIED?

That's right! And that was the fall of man. And so because sin entered into us, we're all born with this little dead spirit lying there.[5]

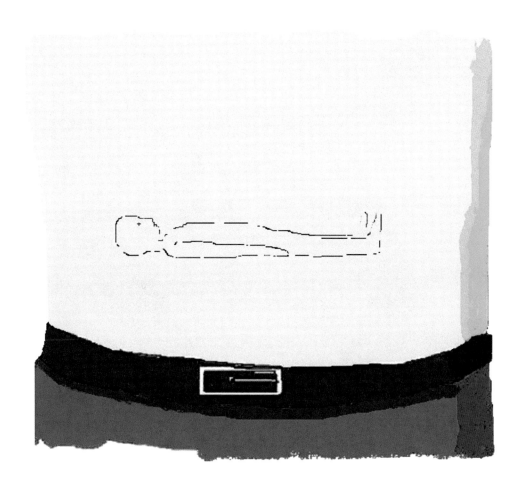

A pure and Holy God cannot fellowship with sin[6] and He missed fellowshipping with His children and so He did something about it.

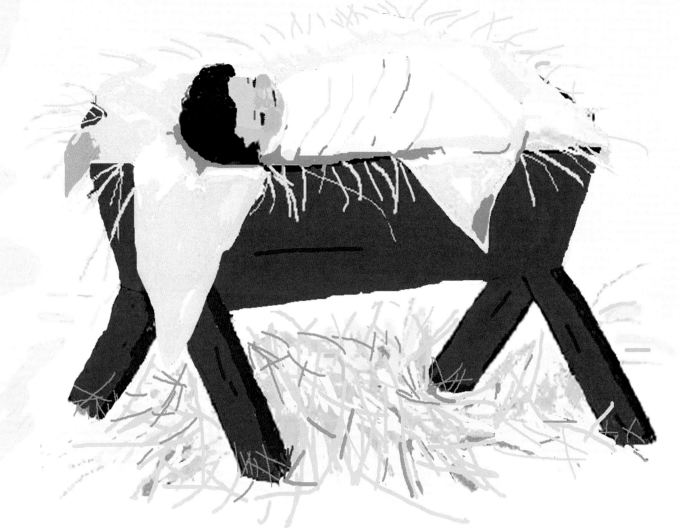

He sent the very best thing He had, His very own Son, to rescue us![7]

To be the Savior
of the world!

Because He loves us so much.

And God's own Blood is the only thing Holy enough to wash away all the sins of the whole world! And so God became a man called Jesus.

And His whole purpose in Life was to get that Holy Blood from that manger to the cross![8]

He did a lot of wonderful things in between.
He did a bunch of miracles
to prove He was God.[9]

And He taught many wonderful things, but it just made a lot of people mad.[10]

So they put Him on the cross, but He wasn't surprised. And when those nails went in and that Holy Blood came out, that paid the price for all the sins of the whole world![11]

And so all we have to do is to believe with all our hearts that Jesus is the Savior of the world.

And that He died on the cross
to pay for our sins.

And that He
was laid in a tomb
and on the
third day
He rose again![12]

And we ask Him to forgive us of
all our sins and to wash our
sins away with His Holy Blood.

And we ask Him to come into our hearts
and He sends His Holy...

That's right!

So He comes in and joins
with our little dead spirit
and He wakes it up.[13] And
we become BORN AGAIN![14]

And now we can fellowship once again with God Spirit to Spirit! And that's what's going to heaven![15]

And that's what it means to be
BORN AGAIN!

You can be BORN AGAIN too!
Would you like to pray now?

Dear Father, please forgive me of all my sins. Come into my heart and wash me and cleanse me with your Holy Blood. And fill me up with your Holy Spirit and make me brand new. I give my life to you now. I believe I am Born Again and I will live in Heaven with you forever. Thank you for saving me. In Jesus' name, Amen.

If you just prayed that prayer,
the Bible says that you have become
a brand new person![16] And now you can
fellowship with your heavenly Father
and you have become a member of His
wonderful family called
the Body of Christ![17]

Isn't that wonderful?

THE END

Or should we say,

THE BEGINNING

Tempe Brown is a native of Oklahoma.
She is an artist, an author, a songwriter and singer.
She is an inspirational speaker and speaks for various
organizations, churches and conferences.
To learn more about her,
visit her website at tempebrown.org.

ENDNOTES

1 John 4:24: "God is Spirit, and those who worship Him must worship in spirit and truth."

2 Genesis 2:7: "And the LORD God formed man [of] the dust of the ground, and breathed into his nostrils the breath of life; and man became a living being."

3 Genesis 2:16, 17: "And the LORD God commanded the man, saying, 'Of every tree of the garden you may freely eat; "but of the tree of the knowledge of good and evil you shall not eat, for in the day that you eat of it you shall surely die.' "

4 Genesis 3:1-6: "Now the serpent was more cunning than any beast of the field which the LORD God had made. And he said to the woman, 'Has God indeed said, 'You shall not eat of every tree of the garden'? And the woman said to the serpent, 'We may eat the fruit of the trees of the garden; but of the fruit of the tree which is in the midst of the garden, God has said, 'You shall not eat it, nor shall you touch it, lest you die.' Then the serpent said to the woman, 'You will not surely die. For God knows that in the day you eat of it your eyes will be opened, and you will be like God, knowing good and evil.' So when the woman saw that the tree was good for food, that it was pleasant to the eyes, and a tree desirable to make one wise, she took of its fruit and ate. She also gave to her husband with her, and he ate."

5 Romans 6:23 "For the wages of sin is death, but the gift of God is eternal life in Christ Jesus our Lord."

  Romans 5:12: "Therefore, just as through one man sin entered the world, and death through sin, and thus death spread to all men, because all sinned."

6 I John 1:6: "If we say that we have fellowship with Him, and walk in darkness, we lie and do not practice the truth."

7 John 3:16: "For God so loved the world that He gave His only begotten Son, that whoever believes in Him should not perish but have everlasting life."

8 I John 1:7: "But if we walk in the light as He is in the light, we have fellowship with one another, and the blood of Jesus Christ His Son cleanses us from all sin."

9 Matthew 4:23; 8:3, 16; 9:35; 12:13, 22; 14:36; 15:30; 17:18;19:2 ; 21:14; Mark 1:31; 10:52; Luke 7:21; 13:13; 17:14; 22:51: John 4:50; 5:9; 9:6

10 Luke 4:9; 23:11; John 5:16; 7:1; 8:37; 10:39

11 Revelation 1:5: "And from Jesus Christ, the faithful witness, the firstborn from the dead, and the ruler over the kings of the earth. To Him who loved us and washed us from our sins in His own blood."

12 I Corinthians 15: 3, 4: "For I delivered to you first of all that which I also received: that Christ died for our sins according to the Scriptures, and that He was buried, and that He rose again the third day according to the Scriptures."

13 I Peter 1:3: "Blessed be the God and Father of our Lord Jesus Christ, who according to His abundant mercy has begotten us again to a living hope through the resurrection of Jesus Christ from the dead."

14 John 3:3: "Jesus answered and said to him, "Most assuredly, I say to you, unless one is born again, he cannot see the kingdom of God."

15 I John 1:3: "That which we have seen and heard we declare to you, that you also may have fellowship with us; and truly our fellowship [is] with the Father and with His Son Jesus Christ."

16 II Corinthians 5:17: "Therefore, if anyone is in Christ, he is a new creation; old things have passed away; behold, all things have become new."

17 I Corinthians 12:12: "For as the body is one and has many members, but all the members of that one body, being many, are one body, so also is Christ."

Made in the USA
Columbia, SC
25 October 2020